What are WORDS, Really?

written by Alexi Lubomirski   illustrated by Carlos Aponte

CANDLEWICK PRESS

What are

Words can be funny, like

PLINKETY PLONK

OR STINKEDY STINKSON

or HIPPOPOTAMY

HONK

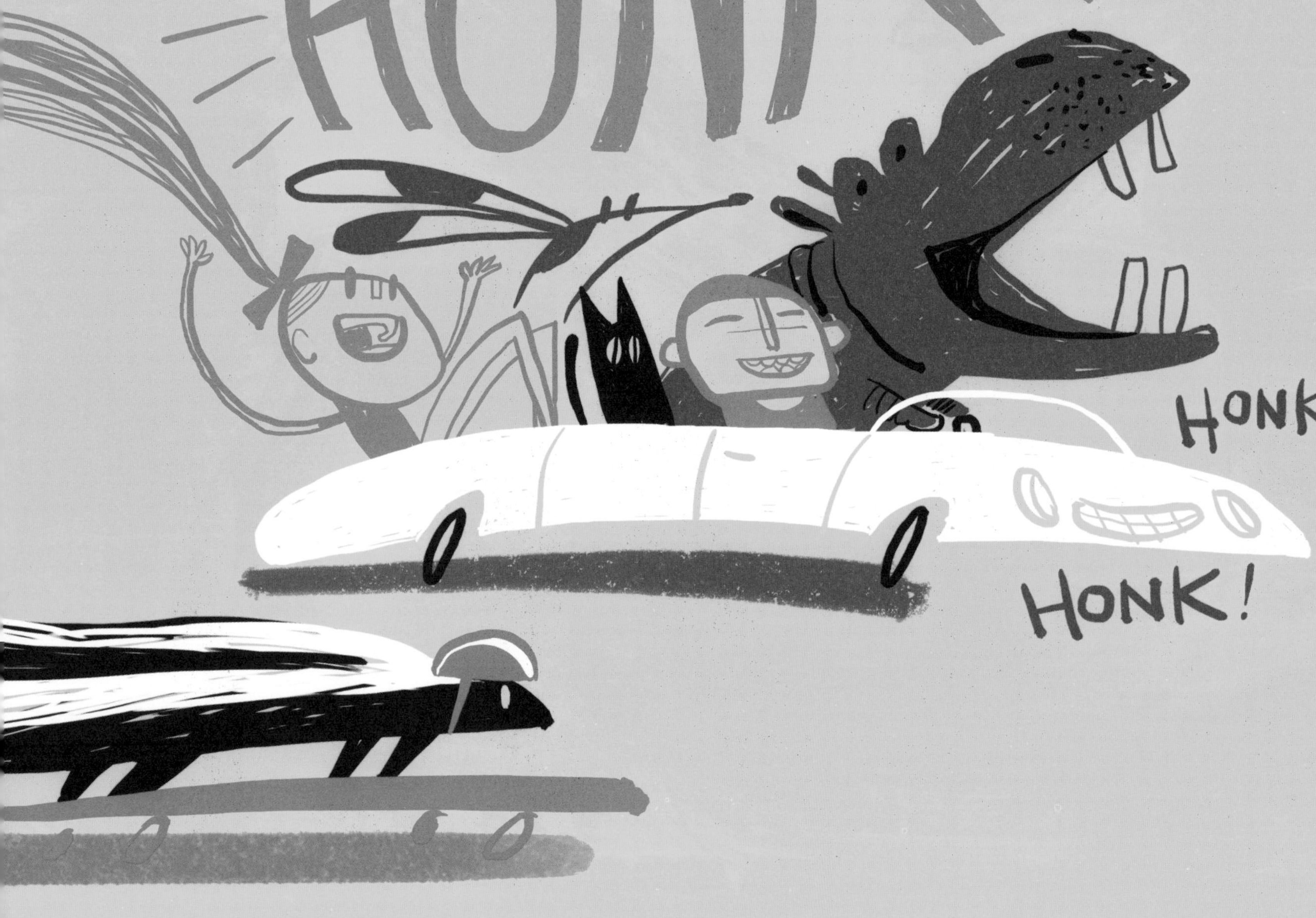

BUT WORDS can also cause Pain, LiKe

or

DumB,

and make
you feel unhappy,
less than, or glum.

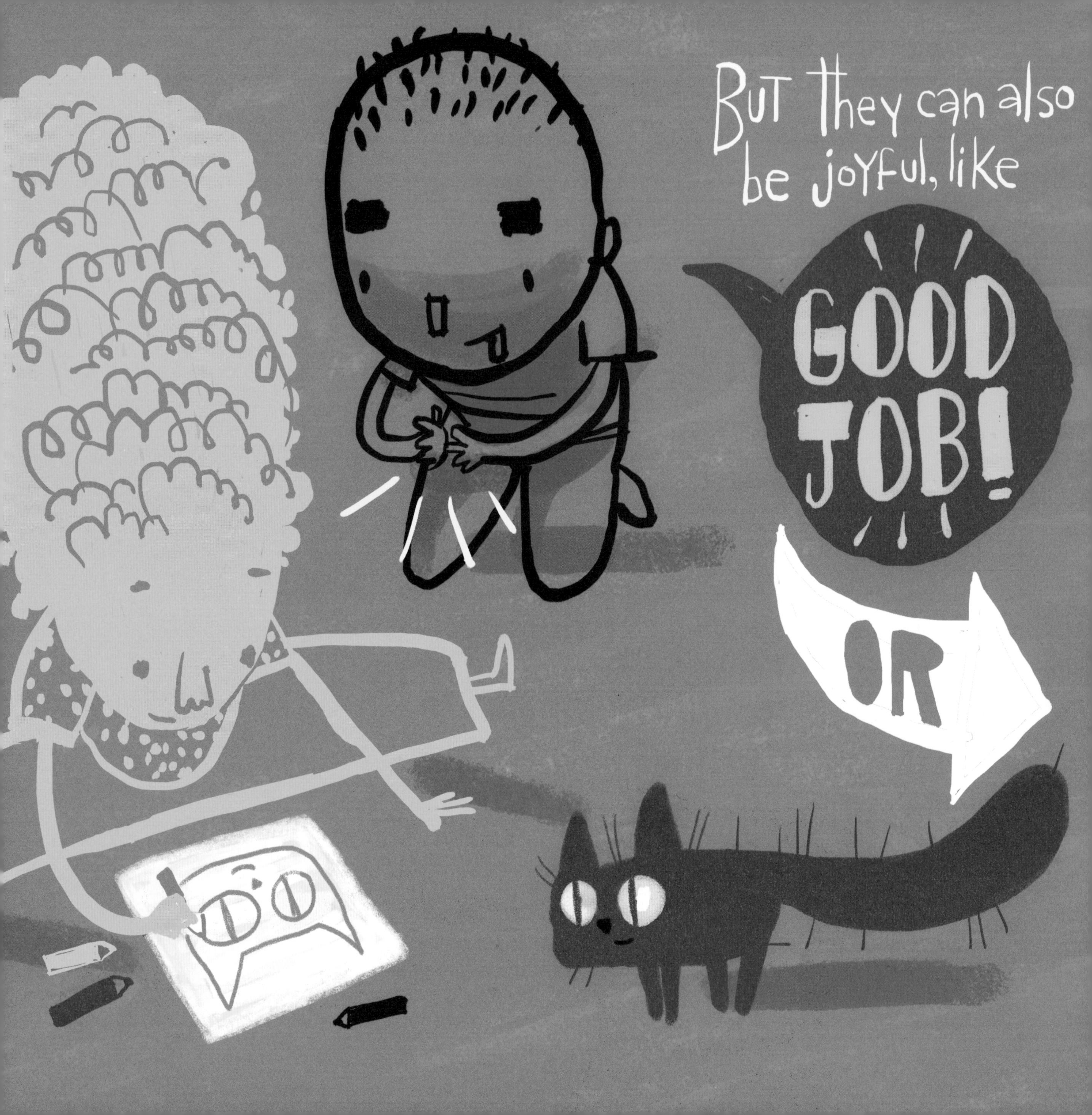
But they can also be joyful, like
GOOD JOB!
OR

WAHOO!

and can make you jump **higher** than a **laughing kangaroo!**

So let's look at two words that each have four letters.

One is

HATE.

One is LOve.

Which one makes you feel better?

can make you feel as high as the sky!

Now, consider how your **words** can affect **EVERYTHING** that surrounds you!
You can make **life** amazing.
Go ahead, look around you!

Let's try an experiment,

and see if your life gets better

where you change what you **say**

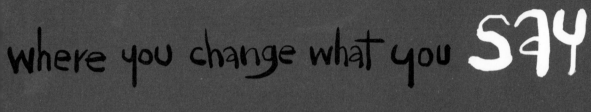

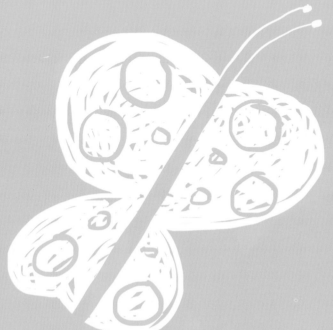

in a **Wonderful** way.

Like a Magical spell

from a

wizard

or elf,

Just repeating positive words can change your state of mind, like swapping

I am worthless for

i am unique

or

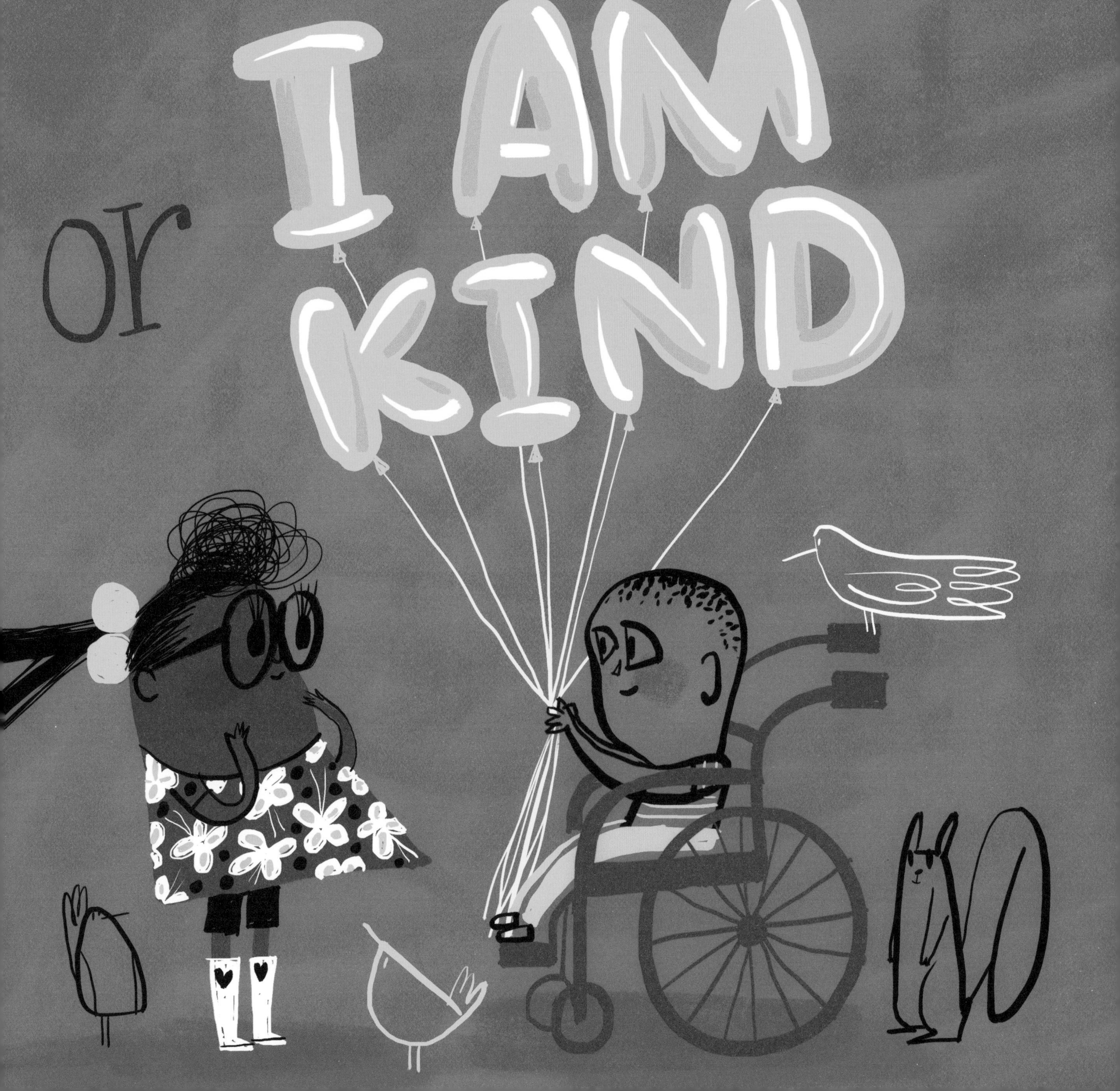

And if you think something nice about a person, don't be shy! **TELL THEM!** They may need to hear it, even if you don't quite know why.

SO start

considering each WORD AND ITS

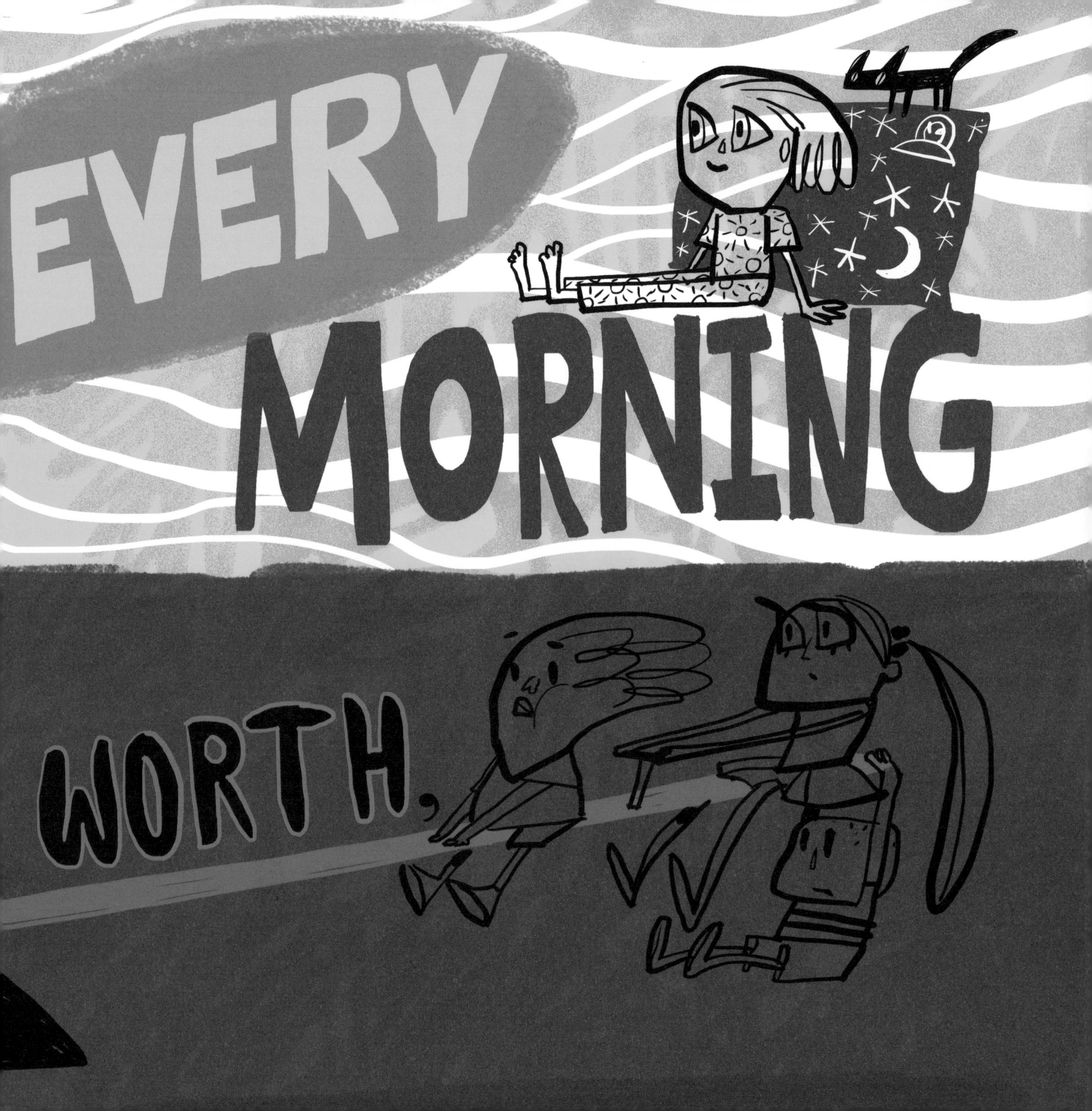
EVERY MORNING
WORTH,

I LOVE YOU.

Dedicated to my sons, Sole Luka and Leone,
and their endless imaginations
AL

To the world I know—
every day is an opportunity to do better
CA

First edition 2022

Library of Congress Catalog Card Number pending
ISBN 978-1-5362-1980-7

22 23 24 25 26 27 APS 10 9 8 7 6 5 4 3 2 1

Printed in Humen, Dongguan, China

The illustrations in this book were created digitally.

Candlewick Press
99 Dover Street
Somerville, Massachusetts 02144

www.candlewick.com